Vivid Beauty
WOMEN OF THE WORLD COLORING BOOK
Illustrated by
Pamela Duarte

Vivid Beauty: Women of the World Coloring Book
©2018 Pamela Duarte

Celebrate your strength, beauty, and creativity!

©2018 Pamela Duarte

"Here's to strong women! May we know them. May we be them. May we raise them."
-Unknown

This book is dedicated to:

Richard Ellescas:
my teacher, my mentor, &, most importantly, a wonderful friend.

About This Book

This book was created to celebrate the strength, beauty, & creativity of women.

I've been inspired by the many colorists around the world who post & express their talent daily.

It is titled "Vivid Beauty" because I felt the definition fit the art of colorists so well:

1. Strikingly bright or intense, as color, light, etc.
2. Full of life; lively; animated
3. Presenting the appearance, freshness, spirit, etc., of life
4. Strong, distinct, or clearly perceptible
5. Forming distinct and striking mental images

I have illustrated 25 different designs, each of which are printed twice in case you would like to try a different color scheme. There is also a Color Palette Test Page in the back.

The pages of this book are suitable for colored pencils, markers, and a variety of other media. They are only printed on one side but, to help prevent bleed through, place a blank sheet of paper between the pages when coloring.

Please let your imagination be your guide!

These illustrations are for personal use only.

©2018 Pamela Duarte

©2018 Pamela Duarte

©2018 Pamela Duarte

©2018 Pamela Duarté

©2018 Pamela Duarte

©2018 Pamela Duarte

©2018 Pamela Duarte

©2018 Pamela Duarte

©2018 Pamela Duarte

©2018 Pamela Duarté

©2018 Pamela Duarte

©2018 Pamela Duarte

©2018 Pamela Duarte

©2018 Pamela Duarté

©2018 Pamela Duarté

©2017 Pamela Duarté

©2017 Pamela Duarte

©2018 Pamela Duarte

©2018 Pamela Duarté

©2018 Pamela Duarte

©2018 Pamela Duarté

©2018 Pamela Duarté

©2018 Pamela Duarte

©2018 Pamela Duarté

©2018 Pamela Duarté

©2017 Pamela Duarte

©2017 Pamela Duarte

©2017 Pamela Duarte

©2017 Pamela Duarte

©2018 Pamela Duarte

©2018 Pamela Duarte

©2018 Pamela Duarté

©2018 Pamela Duarte

©2017 Pamela Duarte

©2017 Pamela Duarte

©2018 Pamela Duarte

©2018 Pamela Duarte

©2018 Pamela Duarte

©2018 Pamela Duarte

©2018 Pamela Duarté

©2018 Pamela Duarte

©2017 Pamela Duarté

©2017 Pamela Duarte

©2018 Pamela Duarte

©2018 Pamela Duarte

©2018 Pamela Duarte

©2018 Pamela Duarté

About The Artist

Pamela Duarte received a BFA from Art Center College of Design. After graduation she worked as a fashion illustrator and then segued into fashion dolls. She has worked on projects for many companies including Mattel Toys where she has illustrated Barbie and other products. She has also designed for toy companies in Hong Kong.

She loves to travel and has lived in Los Angeles, New York, and Bali. She currently lives in the peaceful Ojai Valley.

Other books by Pamela Duarte:
Flower Mandalas Coloring Book
Flower Patterns Coloring Book, Volume 1
Flower Patterns Coloring Book, Volume 2
Flowers & Fashion: Women of the World Coloring Book

These illustrations are for personal use only.

Color Palette Test Page